The American Mosaic
Immigration Today

Immigrants' Rights, Citizens' Rights

Sara Howell

PowerKiDS press™

New York

Published in 2015 by The Rosen Publishing Group, Inc.
29 East 21st Street, New York, NY 10010

First Edition

Editors: Jennifer Way and Norman D. Graubart
Book Design: Andrew Povolny
Photo Research: Katie Stryker

Photo Credits: Cover Hill Street Studios/Blend Images/Getty Images; p. 4 Olaf Speier/Shutterstock.com; p. 5 Boston Globe/Getty Images; p. 6 Pete Spiro/Shutterstock.com; p. 7 monkeybusinessimages/iStock/Thinkstock; p. 9 Monkey Business Images/Shutterstock.com; p. 10 Epoxydude/Getty Images; p. 11 Ryan Rodrick Beiler/Shutterstock.com; p. 12 Universal Images Group/Getty Images; p. 13 (top) Zurijeta/Shutterstock.com; p. 13 (bottom) Rob Marmion/Shutterstock.com; p. 14 moodboard/Thinkstock; p. 15 Handout/Getty Images News/Getty Images; pp. 16–17 PBNJ Productions/Blend Images/Getty Images; p. 18 Phototreat/iStock/Thinkstock; p. 19 Blend Images - Hill Street Studios/Brand X Images/Getty Images; p. 20 Fuse/Thinkstock; p. 21 Sisse Brimberg/National Geographic/Getty Images; p. 22 Radius Images/Getty Images

Library of Congress Cataloging-in-Publication Data

Howell, Sara.
Immigrants' rights, citizens' rights / by Sara Howell. — First Edition.
    pages cm. — (The American mosaic : immigration today)
Includes index.
ISBN 978-1-4777-6739-9 (library binding) —
ISBN 978-1-4777-6740-5 (pbk.) — ISBN 978-1-4777-6647-7 (6-pack)
1. United States—Emigration and immigration—Government policy
—Juvenile literature. 2. Emigration and immigration law—United States
—Juvenile literature. 3. Immigrants—United States—Juvenile literature.
4. Citizenship—United States—Juvenile literature. I. Title.
JV6483.H68 2015
323.0973—dc23
                                    2014002374

Manufactured in the United States of America

CPSIA Compliance Information: Batch #WS14PK1: For Further Information contact Rosen Publishing, New York, New York at 1-800-237-9932

Contents

Who Are Immigrants and Citizens?

There are about 314 million people in the United States today. These people have many different cultures, religions, and backgrounds. Most of the people living in the United States are **citizens**. This means they were born here or have a legal right to live in this country.

This cheese maker is a recent immigrant. Immigrants work all kinds of different jobs in America.

This is a citizenship naturalization ceremony. All of the people in this picture are about to become American citizens.

More than 40 million people in the United States are **immigrants**. An immigrant is a person who moves from one country to another. Some immigrants choose to apply for citizenship. Once they become citizens, they can enjoy the same rights as those who were born in the United States!

Natural-Born Citizens

In the United States, there are two ways to become a citizen. The first is to be born here. This is often called natural-born citizenship. People born in the United States do not need to do anything to become citizens. In fact, they are citizens even if their parents are not.

All babies born in American hospitals are American citizens. The Fourteenth Amendment to the Constitution gives citizenship to all people born in America.

Kids who are born to American parents in South Korea, Italy, or any other country are also American citizens. In military families, children are often born overseas.

Some natural-born citizens were actually born in other countries. However, if one or both of their parents were US citizens, then they are citizens, too. For example, members of the US military often serve in other countries. Their children are US citizens, no matter where they are born.

Citizens by Law

The second way to become a US citizen is to become one by law. This is called **naturalization**. Immigrants in the United States may apply to become naturalized citizens.

Immigrants may take different paths to citizenship. In general, an immigrant must enter the United States legally. He must then live here as a **permanent resident** for at least five years. The US government will check the immigrant's background to be sure he has not been in trouble with the law. Immigrants also must prove they can speak and understand English and understand how the US government works.

Applying for citizenship is a long and difficult process. However, once a person is granted naturalized citizenship, he or she has the same rights and responsibilities as a natural-born citizen!

Types of Immigrants

This is a permanent-resident card, or green card. Not all American immigrants have one, but those who do have more rights under the law than those who don't.

Most immigrants who live in the United States are here legally. This means they have immigrant **visas**, or permanent-resident cards. These give them permission to live and work in the United States. Each year, only a certain number of immigrant visas are given to people from each country around the world. Today, large numbers of legal immigrants come to the United States from Mexico, China, India, and the Philippines.

Of the 40 million immigrants living in the United States, about 12 million are here illegally. These people are often called **undocumented** immigrants. They do not have permission to work, though many do.

Some Americans have worked to give undocumented immigrants more rights.

What Are Rights?

A right is something that people should be able to do. People who live in the United States have many important rights. The most important of these are found in the Bill of Rights. This is the first 10 amendments, or changes, to the Constitution.

James Madison was the main author of the Bill of Rights. He would later become the fourth president of the United States.

These Muslim students are allowed to practice their religion freely. This is one of the rights guaranteed by the First Amendment.

Most rights in the United States apply to both citizens and immigrants. For example, both have the right to freedom of speech. This right lets people say or write what they believe without fear of getting in trouble with the US government. People also have the right to belong to any religion they choose.

During the citizenship application process, there will be an interview. This is a good time to discuss what you like about America, such as our constitutional rights.

Rights of Citizens

This is a jury in an American courtroom. In criminal trials, a jury decides whether someone is guilty or innocent.

In the United States, citizens enjoy all the rights listed in the Constitution. They have the right to vote in **elections** and decide who will serve them in the US government. They have the right to be judged by **juries** if they are accused of crimes. They also have the right to serve on juries in the trials of others.

In most cases, both natural-born citizens and naturalized citizens hold all the same rights. However, the Constitution gives natural-born citizens one special right. It says a person must be a natural-born citizen to serve as the US president.

President Barack Obama was born in Hawaii in 1961. This means he is a natural-born citizen.

Rights of Immigrants

All US citizens and all immigrants have the right to emergency medical care. This includes undocumented immigrants.

Both documented and undocumented immigrants have many important rights. For example, all immigrants have the right to be protected by the laws of the United States. This means no one is allowed to hurt them or steal from them because they are not citizens. The children of all immigrants have the right to go to public school and get a good education.

Documented immigrants also have the right to serve in the US military. This can provide them with special training and help them get other jobs. It can also help them if they choose to apply for citizenship.

Deportation

The Border Patrol guards America's borders. Sometimes, its agents catch undocumented immigrants trying to cross the border. These people are often deported.

Citizens of the United States have the right to live here as long as they choose. However, permanent residents and undocumented immigrants can sometimes be forced to leave the United States and return to the country from which they came. This is called **deportation**.

There are many reasons why people may be deported. They may have entered the country illegally or with falsified, or fake, documents. They may have committed a very serious crime or many minor crimes. An immigrant can also be deported for illegally voting in an election.

Because the United States is a democracy, voting is one of our most important rights. Immigrants cannot vote in elections until they become citizens.

Rights and Crime

Some rights listed in the Constitution help people accused of crimes, no matter what their immigration status is. These rights can help people prove their innocence. They also help keep the legal system fair. People have the right to be helped in their defense by a lawyer.

This lawyer is arguing her case to a jury. Every person who is arrested in the United States has the right to a lawyer, even if he cannot afford one.

Migrant workers come to America for a short time to do certain jobs. Some migrant workers are undocumented, but they are protected by American labor laws.

If a court decides that a person is guilty of a crime, he still has many important rights. People in prison have the right to be treated **humanely**. The Constitution's Eighth Amendment says people in prison cannot be punished in cruel and unusual ways.

A Cultural Mosaic

In some parts of the world, people do not have many rights. The freedoms that citizens and immigrants enjoy help make the United States the country that it is.

We can think of the United States as a **mosaic**. A mosaic is a picture made by fitting many small pieces together to create a larger work. The people who live here, whether they are citizens or immigrants, come from different backgrounds and cultures. However, they fit together with others around them to create a larger American picture!

Immigrants from all around the world come to America to be a part of our cultural mosaic. Where does your family come from?

Glossary

citizens (SIH-tih-zenz) People who were born in or have a right to all the rights and protections of a country.

deportation (dee-por-TAY-shun) The act of sending someone out of a country.

elections (ee-LEK-shunz) Choosing people for positions by voting for them.

humanely (hyoo-MAYN-lee) Kindly or in a way that does not cause pain.

immigrants (IH-muh-grunts) People who move to a new country from another country.

juries (JOOR-eez) Groups of people chosen to make decisions in court cases based on the facts given to them.

mosaic (moh-ZAY-ik) A picture made by fitting together small pieces of stone, glass, or tile and pasting them in place.

naturalization (na-chuh-ruh-luh-ZAY-shun) The process of becoming a citizen.

permanent resident (PER-muh-nint REH-zih-dent) A person who is not a citizen but who has the right to live and work in a country forever.

undocumented (un-DO-kyuh-ment-ed) Not having the official papers that allow one to live and work in a country legally.

visas (VEE-zuz) Official permission to enter a country.

Index

Websites

Due to the changing nature of Internet links, PowerKids Press
has developed an online list of websites related to the subject
of this book. This site is updated regularly. Please use this link
to access the list:

www.powerkidslinks.com/mosa/immri/